To

Eric & Clarissa

From

mother & Dad Bontreger

Date

Easter   2010

WITH **WINGS** LIKE **EAGLES**

PAINTINGS BY
THE HAUTMAN BROTHERS

HARVEST HOUSE PUBLISHERS

EUGENE, OREGON

But those who wait on the LORD
Shall renew their strength;
They shall mount up with wings like eagles,
They shall run and not be weary,
They shall walk and not faint.

ISAIAH 40:31 NKJV

CONTENTS

One can never consent to creep when one feels an impulse to soar.

HELEN KELLER

FREEDOM TO FLY

With remarkable ease, the eagle soars high above the dwellings of humans and the confines of the earth. What a gift is when on a sunny afternoon you tilt your head to the sky and notice this majestic bird journeying the blue with strength and grace. It's impossible to look away when you witness freedom. With your hand held up to your brow to shade your eyes, you track this vision of God's artistry in flight. Notice how the bird's wings barely move as it relies on the breeze highways to carry it great distances. It gives itself over to the rush of wind that is orchestrated by its Maker.

When you take in such a sight, your heart feels as if it has wings that have spread in unison with those of the incredible creature above. Your heart was made to rest in the power of God, to trust His guiding strength, and to experience the wondrous journey of discovery.

Without faith a man can do nothing; with it all things are possible.

SIR WILLIAM OSLER

Go forth under the open sky,
and list
To Nature's teachings.

WILLIAM CULLEN BRYANT

All things are engaged in writing their history. The planet, the pebble, goes attended by its shadow. The rolling rock leaves its scratches on the mountain; the river, its channel in the soil; the animal, its bones in the stratum; the fern and leaf, their modest epitaph in the coal. The falling drop makes its sculpture in the sand or the stone. Not a foot steps into the snow or along the ground, but prints, in characters more or less lasting, a map of its march. Every act of the man inscribes itself in the memories of its fellows, and in his own manners and face. The air is full of sounds, the sky of tokens, the ground is all memoranda and signatures, and every object covered over with hints which speak to the intelligent.

RALPH WALDO EMERSON

To give thanks in solitude is enough. Thanksgiving has wings and goes where it must go. Your prayer knows much more about it than you do.

VICTOR HUGO

Does the eagle soar at your command
and build his nest on high? He dwells
on a cliff and stays there at night;
a rocky crag is his stronghold.

JOB 39:27-28

Be inspired with the belief that life is a great and noble calling;
not a mean and groveling thing that we are to shuffle through
as we can, but an elevated and lofty destiny.

WILLIAM E. GLADSTONE

The wild bird that flies so lone and far has somewhere its nest
and brood. A little fluttering heart of love impels its wings, and
points its course.

EDWIN HUBBELL CHAPIN

Glad with Thy light, and glowing with Thy love,

So let me ever speak and think and move

As fits a soul new-touched with life from Heaven,

That seeks but so to order all her course

As most to show the glory of that Source

By Whom her strength, her hope, her life are given.

C.J.P. SPITTA

VISION AND HOPE

Eagles are known for their keen vision. Not only can they see more than twice as far as we can, they also are able to perceive more colors. When they survey the world below, they can spot their lunch two miles away or locate the perfect landing strip of a sturdy tree limb. The brilliant eagles are survivors because they can examine horizons that extend far beyond what we could imagine.

God gives us a similar ability—hope. When we discover our hope in God and in our future purpose, it gives us the keen vision of the eagle. We might not see a rabbit half a neighborhood away, but we do start to view life beyond our immediate circumstances. We gain the insight of faith and compassion, and soon we see the beauty of a future even when we face difficulties today. Hope opens our eyes and hearts to a horizon that extends far beyond what we could ever imagine.

*Nature and truth are one, and immutable, and inseparable
 as beauty and love.*

MRS. ANNA BROWNELL JAMESON

*Hope is the thing with feathers
That perches in the soul.*

EMILY DICKINSON

*Now all the knowledge and wisdom that is in creatures, wheth-
angels or men, is nothing else but a participation of that one
eternal, immutable and increased wisdom of God.*

RALPH J. CUDWORTH

*Every moment is a golden one for him who has the vision to
recognize it as such.*

HENRY MILLER

Will you set your eyes on that which
is not? For riches certainly make
themselves wings; They fly away
like an eagle toward heaven.

PROVERBS 23:5 NKJV

As he that fears God hears nothing else, so, he that sees God sees everything else.

JOHN DONNE

The natural flights of the human mind are not from pleasure to pleasure, but from hope to hope.

SAMUEL JOHNSON

I hear beyond the range of sound,

I see beyond the range of sight,

New earths and skies and seas around,

And in my day the sun doth pale his light.

HENRY DAVID THOREAU

See the enfranchised bird, who wildly springs,

With a keen sparkle in his glowing eye

And a strong effort in his quivering wings,

Up to the blue vault of the happy sky.

LADY CAROLINE SHERIDAN NORTON

I lift up my eyes to the hills—
where does my help come from?
My help comes from the LORD,
the Maker of heaven and earth.

PSALM 121:1-2

u are not here merely to ake a living. You are here to able the world to live more iply, with greater vision, d with a finer spirit of hope d achievement. You are re to enrich the world. You ipoverish yourself if you rget this errand.

Woodrow Wilson

I see my way as birds their trackless way; I shall arrive! What time, what

circuit first, I ask not....He guides me and the bird. In His good time.

ROBERT BROWNING

FAITHFULNESS

Nature abounds with evidence of God's faithfulness. From the dazzle of the new dawn on the crest of a wave to the recurring performance of the stars at night, we need only to take a look around us to sense the reality of our Creator's care. Eagles demonstrate faithfulness in many ways. They are monogamous, nurturing of their young, and they are exceptional nesters. They add to the girth of their nests with such gusto that they can create home bases that weigh several tons. If eagles travel to the south and then back to the north each year, they return to the same places each time.

We express faithfulness in our lives just as eagles do. We are loving and respectful in our relationships, we are consistent and supportive as parents, and we strive to create a home that serves as a solid foundation for our family members. And when we experience distance, it is our sense of home that calls us back to faith and love time after time.

Yet the fresh air of the evening sighs among the leaves; the birds,

those voices of the flowers, repeat the evening prayer.

JEAN-BAPTISTE-CAMILLE COROT

He shielded him and cared for him;
he guarded him as the apple of his eye,
like an eagle that stirs up its nest and
hovers over its young, that spreads
its wings to catch them and
carries them on its pinions.

DEUTERONOMY 32:10-11

Faithfulness springs forth from the earth,
nd righteousness looks down from heaven.

PSALM 85:11

is not the language of painters, but the language of nature which

e should listen to.

INCENT VAN GOGH

he most natural beauty in the world is honesty and moral truth.

or all beauty is truth.

ORD SHAFTESBURY

hen the little Hiawatha

earned of every bird its language,

earned their names and all their secrets,

Iow they built their nests in summer,

Vhere they hid themselves in winter...

HENRY WADSWORTH LONGFELLOW,

Hiawatha's Childhood

And as a bird each fond endearment tries

To tempt its new-fledg'd offspring to the skies,

He tried each art, reprov'd each dull delay,

Allur'd to brighter worlds, and led the way.

OLIVER GOLDSMITH

God writes the gospel not in the Bible alone,

but on trees and flowers and clouds and

stars.

MARTIN LUTHER

Surely there is something in the unruffled calm of nature that overawes our little anxieties and doubts; the sight of the deep-blue sky and the clustering stars above seems to impart a quiet to the mind.

TRYON EDWARDS

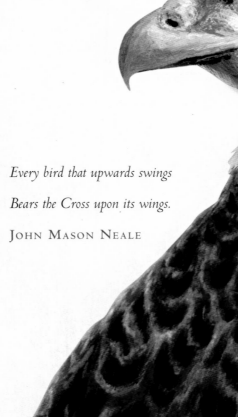

there's a power above us,

nd that there is all nature

es aloud through all her

orks) he must delight in

rtue.

OSEPH ADDISON

King of the peak and glacier,

King of the cold, white scalps,

He lifts his head at that close

tread,

The eagle of the Alps.

VICTOR HUGO

No bird soars too high if he

soars with his own wings.

WILLIAM BLAKE

Cut a path into

The heaven of glory

Leaving a track of light for men

To wonder at.

WILLIAM BLAKE

Every bird that upwards swings

Bears the Cross upon its wings.

JOHN MASON NEALE

ng out my soul, thy songs

of joy;

ich as a happy bird will sing,

eneath a Rainbow's lovely

arch,

early spring.

VILLIAM HENRY DAVIES

There are only two ways to live your life. One is as though nothing

is a miracle. The other is as though everything is a miracle.

ALBERT EINSTEIN

BEAUTY AND WONDER

The regal beauty of the eagle has been admired for centuries. We know the eagle a prominent symbol of America, but ancient cultures so used the likeness of this bird to represent free-om, strength, deity, and power. Some species of the gle are built to maneuver the narrow passages of a ick forest. Others have a broad expanse of wing that lows them to surf the wind for great distances above e open sea. No matter which of its characteristics captures the heart of onlookers, this graceful traveler of the sky commands attention and inspires awe in all.

Like the eagle, we are each blessed with unique gifts that can inspire others to explore and express the beauty and wonder of life. What offers a glimpse of splendor in your attitude and the way you relate to others? When you rise and face the open day ahead, anticipate the gifts and treasures waiting to be discovered. Take in the beauty of living as a unique and amazing creation.

Everybody needs beauty as well as bread, places to play in and pray in, where nature may heal and give strength to body and soul.

JOHN MUIR

Glance at the sun. See the moon and stars. Gaze at the beauty of the green earth. Now think.

HILDEGARD OF BINGEN

Develop interest in life as you see it; in people, things, literature, music—the world is so rich, simply throbbing with rich treasures, beautiful souls. . .

HENRY MILLER

And let the beauty of the LORD our God be upon us, And establish the work of our hands for us.

PSALM 90:17 NKJV

When thou seest an eagle, thou seest a portion of genius; lift up thy head!

WILLIAM BLAKE

Though we travel the world over to find the beautiful, we must carry it with us or we find it not.

RALPH WALDO EMERSON

My heart is awed within me when I think
Of the great miracle that still goes on,
In silence, round me—the perpetual work
Of thy creation, finished, yet renewed
Forever. Written on thy works I read
The lesson of thy own eternity.

WILLIAM CULLEN BRYANT

Beauty is truth—truth, beauty—that is all ye know on earth, and all ye need to know.

JOHN KEATS

All things bright and beautiful,

All creatures great and small,

All things wise and wonderful,

The Lord God made them all.

Each little flower that opens,

Each little bird that sings,

He made their glowing colors,

He made their tiny wings.

...He gave us eyes to see them,

And lips that we might tell,

How great is God Almighty,

Who has made all things well.

CECIL FRANCES ALEXANDE

best thing is to go from nature's God down to nature; and if

once get to nature's God, and believe Him, and love Him, it

urprising how easy it is to hear music in the waves, and songs

he wild whisperings of the winds; to see God everywhere

he stones, in the rocks, in the rippling brooks, and hear Him

rywhere, in the lowing of cattle, in the rolling of thunder,

l in the fury of tempests.

HARLES HADDON SPURGEON

racles are not a contradiction of nature. They are only in

tradiction of what we know of nature.

. AUGUSTINE

ature gives to every time and season some beauties of its own;

d from morning to night, as from the cradle to the grave, is but

succession of changes so gentle and easy that we can scarcely

ark their progress.

HARLES DICKENS

The very idea of a bird is a symbol and a suggestion to the poet. A

bird seems to be at the top of the scale, so vehement and intense his life.

. . .The beautiful vagabonds, endowed with every grace, masters of all

climes, and knowing no bounds —how many human aspirations are

realised in their free, holiday-lives —and how many suggestions to

the poet in their flight and song!

JOHN BURROUGHS

Yours, O LORD, is the greatness
and the power and the glory and the
majesty and the splendor, for everything
in heaven and earth is yours.

I CHRONICLES 29:11

Never lose an opportunity of seeing anything that is beautiful; for

beauty is God's handwriting—a wayside sacrament. Welcome

it in every fair face, in every fair sky, in every fair flower.

RALPH WALDO EMERSON

STRENGTH TO SOAR

What difficulties do you face? Are the stormy winds of change rising and gaining speed about you? When we look to the eagle's example, we discover a way of faith and perseverance for these times of trouble. This winged wonder is one of the few birds that will face a storm head on—it will enter the uncertain winds and even the assault of rain. Why? Because when they fly with these phenomenal waves of storm air, they can go higher and farther than during times of peaceful breezes and sunny skies. Not only do they survive such storms, they rise above them and discover new vistas.

When we face the potential pain of an approaching, growing problem, our first thought might be to hide, but let us consider the eagle's victory. If we give ourselves over to God's strength, we too will rise up in our circumstances and survive the storm. And we will be given the chance to see life with a perspective broadened by perseverance, trust, hope, and God's enduring grace.

Bird of the broad and sweeping wing!

Thy home is high in heaven,

Where wide the storms their banners fling,

And the tempest clouds are driven.

JAMES GATES PERCIVAL, "To the Eagle"

For wonderful indeed are all His works,

Pleasant to know, and worthiest to be all

Had in remembrance always with delight;

But what created mind can comprehend

Their number, or the wisdom infinite

That brought them forth, but hid their causes deep?

JOHN MILTON

The miracle, or the power, that elevates the few is to be found in their industry, application, and perseverance under the promptings of a brave, determined spirit.

MARK TWAIN

You are my hiding place; you will protect me from trouble and surround me with songs of deliverance.

PSALM 32:7

There's a quiet harbor somewhere
For the poor a-weary soul.

H.H. BROWNELL

O nature! . . . Enrich me with
the knowledge of thy works;
Snatch me to Heaven.

JAMES THOMSON

It is not because things are
difficult that we do not dare,
it is because we do not dare
that they are difficult.

LUCIUS ANNAEUS SENECA

Amidst the storm they sang,

And the stars heard and the sea;

And the sounding aisles of the dim woods rang

To the anthem of the free!

The ocean eagle soar'd

From his nest by the white wave's form;

And the rocking pines of the forest roar'd

This was their welcome home!

FELICIA DOROTHEA HEMANS,

The Landing of the Pilgrim Fathers in New England

In the vast, and the minute, we see

The unambiguous footsteps of the God,

Who gives its lustre to an insect's wing

And wheels His throne upon the rolling worlds.

WILLIAM COWPER

The path was steep and snowy—the way was hard and cold,

But at last we reached the summit, and it glittered with the gold

Of the sun that had been shining, with a perfect, glowing light

From behind the heavy storm clouds that had turned the day to night

And standing on the summit, we looked down and tried to pray,

For we wished to thank the Father who had kept us on our way;

For the snow and sleet and windstorm were but trifles in the past,

And they made the sunshine brighter when we reached the top at last

MARGARET E. SANGSTER

Nature paints not

In oils, but frescoes the great dome of heaven

With sunsets, and the lovely forms of clouds

And flying vapors.

HENRY WADSWORTH LONGFELLOW

aith is a bird that feels dawn
reaking and sings while it is
ill dark.

SCANDINAVIAN SAYING

ike singing bird in high blue air,
o would I soar, and sing Thee
there.

Nor rain, nor stormy wind can be,
When all the air is full of Thee.

LOSE FROM BRIER

There are joys which long to be ours. God sends ten thousand truths, which come about us like birds seeking inlet; but we are shut up to them, and so they bring us nothing, but sit and sing awhile upon the roof, and then fly away.

HENRY WARD BEECHER

Having chosen our course, without guile and with pure purpose, let us renew our trust in God, and go forward without fear and with manly hearts.

ABRAHAM LINCOLN

You cannot fly like an eagle with the wings of a wren.

HENRY HUDSON

Faith without works is like a bird without wings; though she may hop with her companions on earth, yet she will never fly with them to heaven.

FRANCIS BEAUMONT

Faith is daring the soul to go beyond what the eyes can see.
WILLIAM NEWTON CLARK

Love and desire are the spirit's wings to great deeds.
JOHANN WOLFGANG von GOETHE

Nature is but a name for an effect, whose cause is God.
WILLIAM COWPER

Teach us delight in simple things.
RUDYARD KIPLING

The invariable mark of wisdom is to see the miraculous in the common.

RALPH WALDO EMERSON

… like the bird that, passing on her flight awhile on boughs too light, feels them give way beneath her, and yet sings, knowing that she hath wings.

VICTOR HUGO

… heaven-born, the soul a heavenward course must hold; beyond the world she soars; the wise man, I affirm, can find no rest in that which perishes, nor will he lend his heart to ought that doth time depend.

MICHELANGELO

… open, ye heavens, your living doors; let in the great Creator from his work return'd magnificent, his six days' work, a world!

JOHN MILTON

All serious daring starts from within.

HARRIET BEECHER STOWE

I look out of this window and I think this is a cosmos, this is a huge creation,

this is one small corner of it. The trees and birds and everything else and I'm

part of it. I didn't ask to be put here, I've been lucky in finding myself here.

MORRIS WEST

DELIGHT AND JOY

Imagine what it would be like to experience the delight of flight for even one day. What does it feel like to have the rush of air beneath outstretched wings? Defying gravity and soaring over the swirling colors of the maple trees and spring flowers far below must fill an eagle with great joy. When we watch one of God's creatures reveling in nature's playground of earth and sky, we are reminded of the great joy we can receive when we follow through with our purpose and celebrate our surroundings.

You and your gifts are shaped with love and care by the Creator's hands. May the remarkable span of an eagle's wings be a reminder of the breadth of joy that comes with honoring who you are—one of God's amazing creations. And may you greet each new day as a chance to give pleasure back to God by living with a spirit of hope and joy.

Use the talents you possess, for the woods would be a very silent place if no birds sang except for the best.

HENRY VAN DYKE

In every walk with nature one receives far more than he seeks.

JOHN MUIR

Nature does nothing without purpose or uselessly.

ARISTOTLE

Joys are our wings, sorrows are our spurs.

JEAN PAUL RICHTER

One must ask children and birds how cherries and strawberries taste.

JOHANN WOLFGANG VON GOETHE

And little eagles wave their wings in gold.

ALEXANDER POPE

Reflect upon your present blessings, of which every man has many; not on your past misfortunes, of which all men have some.

CHARLES DICKENS

The sun descending in the west,

The evening star does shine;

The birds are silent in their nest,

And I must seek for mine.

The moon, like a flower

In heaven's high bower,

With silent delight

Sits and smiles on the night.

WILLIAM BLAKE, *Night*

Great are the works of the LORD;
they are pondered by all
who delight in them.

PSALM 111:2

...nd your purpose and fling your life out ...to it; and the loftier your purpose is, the ...ore sure you will be to make the world ...cher with every enrichment of yourself.

HILLIPS BROOKS

Alone with Thee, amid the mystic shadows,
The solemn hush of nature newly born;
Alone with Thee in breathless adoration,
In the calm dew and freshness of the morn.

HARRIET BEECHER STOWE

God is a worker. He has thickly strewn
Infinity with grandeur. God is love;
He yet shall wipe away creation's tears,
And all the worlds shall summer in His smile.

ALEXANDER SMITH

My voice shalt thou hear in the morning, O LORD; in the morning will I direct my prayer unto thee, and will look up.

PSALM 5:3 KJV

The ever varying brilliancy and grandeur of the landscape, and the magnificence of the sky, sun, moon and stars, enter more extensive into the enjoyment of mankind than we, perhaps ever think, or can possibly apprehend, without frequent and extensive investigation. This beauty and splendour of the objects around us, it is ever to be remembered, is not necessary to their existence, nor to what we commonly intend by their usefulness. It is therefore to be regarded as a source of pleasure, gratuitously superinduced upon the general nature of the objects themselves, and in this light, a testimony of the divine goodness, peculiarly affecting.

TIMOTHY DWIGHT

Go confidently in the direction of your dreams! Live the life you've imagined.

HENRY DAVID THOREAU

There is a majesty and mystery in nature.

THOMAS CARLYLE

nocent eyes not ours

re made to look on flowers,

yes of small birds and insects small:

orn after summer morn

he sweet rose on her thorn

pens her bosom to them all.

he least and last of things

hat soar on quivering wings,

Or crawl among the grass blades out of sight

lave just as clear a right

o their appointed portion of delight

s Queens or Kings.

HRISTINA G. ROSSETTI,

hese All Wait Upon Thee

Birds, the free tenants of earth, air, and

ocean,. Their forms all symmetry, their mo-

tions grace;

In plumage, delicate and beautiful,

Thick without burthen, close as fish's scales,

Or loose as full blown poppies on the gale;

With wings that seem as they'd a soul within

them,

They bear their owners with such sweet

enchantment.

JAMES MONTGOMERY

See, through this air, this ocean, and this earth,

All matter quick, and bursting into birth.

Above, how high! progressive life may go!

Around, how wide; how deep extend below!

Vast chain of being! which from God began,

Nature's ethereal, human, angel, man,

Beast, bird, fish, insect, what no eye can see,

No glass can reach, from infinite to Thee,

From Thee to nothing.

ALEXANDER POPE

Who loves not the shady trees,

The smell of flowers, the sound of brooks,

The song of birds, and the hum of bees,

Murmuring in green and fragrant nooks,

The voice of children in the spring,

Along the field-paths wandering?

T. MILLAR